LET IT BE A GOOD LIFE

MEIGHAN KLIPPENSTEIN

 FriesenPress

One Printers Way
Altona, MB R0G 0B0
Canada

www.friesenpress.com

ISBN
978-1-03-919566-0 (Hardcover)
978-1-03-919565-3 (Paperback)
978-1-03-919567-7 (eBook)

1. POETRY, CANADIAN

Distributed to the trade by The Ingram Book Company

"Instructions for living a life:
Pay attention.
Be astonished.
Tell about it."

— Mary Oliver

For everyone who has walked beside me in this life.
For those whom I love fiercely.
For my people who stayed.

Introduction

These poems are a collection of moments that mattered. Some brought me through the depths of darkness, some broke my heart, some healed it, and some helped me shine so brightly I thought I might explode from happiness. Writing has always been my cathartic process to make sense of the ebbs and flows of life. Every lesson, love, loss, intention, rejection, redirection, change, shift, beginning, and ending has its own place. Together they create a whole, a complete experience; one requires the other, and I am grateful for all of it. My hope is that you might be able to find something you need inside of these pages.

Let It Be A Good Life has been in the making for the last five years.

It is an honor to have you here.

Contents

PART I

when it gets dark

how can I tell you that it takes
every ounce of living strength
to fully surrender
into the waves
of what is
when what is
isn't what you wanted
how can I tell you that inside acceptance
you will cry
you will feel your old dreams die
and it is there
where you must find
a way to live with the pain
of your life now, reframed
so you can fully surrender
into the waves
of what is
when what is
isn't what you wanted

am I open or empty
messy or clean
I thought it would be easier
to let the sadness pour
out
of
me

releasing grief

precipice
what a beautiful word
for the edge of something
so treacherous

with the wind humming your name
you can't help but lean forward
looking for the light below
she entices you
what does it feel like to fall?
to fly?

the ground beneath your feet gives way
answering the questions inside of your mind
showing you
just how long the way down
truly is

there are times
I am surprised
at the dark inside
at its strength and
how deep its roots can be
the kind you only see
shocked with disbelief
how much it can weave
itself around everything else

suffocating

MEIGHAN KLIPPENSTEIN

I am watching the wind blow
hard enough to bend the trees
so much they almost break

I think to myself
I know that feeling
I know that feeling

when the seasons of change
test my strength to remain standing
and my ability to let go
like how the now bare trees
release their leaves
without question

I take no pleasure in rewinding my mind
back to all those years of just surviving
when I could have been thriving
deep diving
into possibility
of all it meant to be
little and free

you get what you get

MEIGHAN KLIPPENSTEIN

she allowed her pain
to create a reality
that wasn't meant for me
I tried to change it
reframe it
anything to make it
stop raining
all those the days
living with her pain
it held me down
I was a child
I couldn't stop myself from drowning
It's astounding
how could no one step in
how could no one know where to begin
It's astounding
those years compounding
didn't kill me

your eyes locked with mine
you knew exactly where to find
the place I have been searching for
all my life

where the light lives

MEIGHAN KLIPPENSTEIN

I am so tired of hearing
"you turned out so great despite everything"
it is not endearing
you did nothing to steer me
away from the pain
you saw so clearly
my childhood was not easy
all you did was wearily
hope for the best

I learnt how to save myself

before I am awake
the blue from my eyes dissolves
inward falling
the ocean calling
as I sink into the day
a white flag is being raised
effortlessly without question
this place
this familiar state
my mind likes to frequent
unrelenting reflection
that sometimes feels like sorrow swimming

uncovering the window
helped me realize
I had already found
more light this morning
than all of my yesterdays combined

depression lingers

when I was little
I didn't know where to find the joy
it was hidden, overridden
by the darkness that came in
with the pain that wasn't mine
a childhood untied
it's hard to write this
these memories are not priceless
they came at the cost
of everything I lost
when I was little
I didn't know where to find the joy

to feel everything deeply
is not glorious
it is not exciting
it is not a gift
it is exhausting
it is effortless
it is endlessly
learning the new places
each feeling carves into your being
it is knowing
pure anguish and ecstasy
and how it hollows you
wholly

is it possible
to touch another's heart
without leaving a mark
we either hold too tight
or barely at all
it's this kind of carelessness
that should not be mistaken for fearlessness
oh, do we forget
all that we regret
and how we have the power
to hurt those we hold
when will we learn
we have no business reaching toward
another's heart
until we know how
to hold our own

the other side of this season
isn't merry or bright
for those who are struggling
it magnifies

all
that
aches
inside

it doesn't make sense
even when
you are the absolute best
version of yourself

dating

MEIGHAN KLIPPENSTEIN

the loneliness that lives inside of me
does not try to hide from me
it exudes its vibrancy
insistently reminding me
solitude does not always tread lightly

when the darkness caught up
those moments of waking up
were sometimes enough
to make me want to give up
so I started to celebrate
the years of consistency
even though the years felt
like this wasn't how it was meant to be

you'll learn how to sweep away the debris
you'll see

MEIGHAN KLIPPENSTEIN

I didn't know
I wouldn't handle it well
I couldn't tell
how potent
the pain of the past could still be
how it could turn to anger
faster than I could breathe
suffocating the present moment
right out of me
a sharp reminder
of how loss never leaves you

I didn't know
I couldn't have known
I wouldn't handle it well

this is how I come to terms
with loss
I long
to decipher
to recognize
meaning in words
taken from moments anticipated
that have long since dissipated
an experience still awaited
a love that stays

MEIGHAN KLIPPENSTEIN

when the pain arrives
the kind that makes it hard to open the blinds
to see
to be
alive
you will forget everything you ever learnt
about grieving
healing
your heart you can't feel it beating
inside your chest

when the pain arrives
the kind that makes it hard to breathe
to eat
to be
alive
people will remind you of everything you ever learnt
about grieving
healing
so for a moment fleeting
you can start feeling
anything else

when the pain arrives, so do the people

everything we needed to know
we learnt in stages
it wasn't just different pages
it was never the same language
you wanted to roam alone
I wanted to build a home
oh the anguish
it felt dangerous
the kind of pain that came
that day
our views of life collided
we divided
we took everything apart
we broke each other's hearts

we burnt that bridge

MEIGHAN KLIPPENSTEIN

holding my life in reverence
my mind now quiet enough to hear
her softly spoken words
while unknowingly overflowing
my tears fall into my lap
as I am reminded of everything
the longest year contained
the kind of harshness
that made it hard to see
all of the goodness that was given
and still
I bow my head with gratitude
for all the things I have not lost
for all the things I have found

as the days turned into years
to me it was always clear
we were the kind of effortless
you only get after a lifetime
here's the downside
I used it as a lifeline
as some kind of disguise
just to get by
just to hide
the relationship dying
it was only amplifying
the pain that came
knowing effortless wasn't enough

what do you do with the pieces of a broken heart?
hold them in your hands, and
let them sink you
let them bring you
down, allow yourself
to keep on drowning
in the should haves
would haves
if only you could haves
hold them in your hands, and
let them reach you
let them teach you
how
to save yourself
let them sink you
until you learn
until you learn

do you ever wonder why
there are times you can no longer find
a face you recognize
looking back at you in the mirror

I think it's loss

how it ages you
how it changes you
your soul
your bones
your being, and
all you can do is stand there
holding your own hand there
while re-introducing yourself
to the new face in the mirror

MEIGHAN KLIPPENSTEIN

I spent so many years chasing
trying to replace
loneliness with love
what a revelation
learning those aching places
oh how life changed
when I started facing them
life itself explained
there is no exchanging
there is only rearranging
I needed life to break me
it is how I learnt
somebody else could never have saved me

let it in
let it go
that version of life you held onto so
tightly
this memory, that moment
each one ever potent
breathe it in
breathe it out
you must remind yourself
all of that pain, it can't stay
let it in
let it go
take everything you know
and move forward, toward
the new life that is calling
so let it in
and let it go

MEIGHAN KLIPPENSTEIN

the cracks
are not the ending
they are the opening
the beginning, the invitation
to reveal what keeps you heavy

share the weight

the moment I understood
the pain I have been carrying
is not mine
but your darkness disguised
in a single moment
being alive
became redefined
a lifetime of letting go
in one night
I can't tell you how much I cried
how good it felt to realize
my life belongs in the sunshine

I want you to remember
when your heart breaks
it is necessary to sit
in the discomfort
in the uncertainty
in the acceptance
that you had to learn the lessons
I know
it feels like death came in
I want you to remember
it's just another chance to begin
again
again
again

PART II

find the light

I have always loved
a sea of yellow flowers
the way they tower above me
never hiding their tallness
they tell me
it is necessary
to take up space
when searching for the light

if you looked into my soul
you would see
the depth of the ocean
the loyalty of the tides entwined
with the brightest day
the darkest night
vast hope
insatiable curiosity
I interpret it to be

pure
expansive
love

MEIGHAN KLIPPENSTEIN

I love the moments
when I notice
I am finding myself
in places
that were never part of the plan

the only guarantee
I've ever seen
is everything breaks
everything changes
at times without explanation
but it's those life situations
that help you see
freedom is synonymous with let it be

MEIGHAN KLIPPENSTEIN

life makes you wait
until you are ready
I can't explain it
that feeling you get
when you open your eyes
when everything aligns
when you finally find
your people
your soul knows
the relationship flows
an organic beginning
it leaves your head spinning
you just know
they're here to help you grow
a lifetime already underway
it's a lucky day
when you find your people

this isn't your only chance
at happiness
think of all the times you've found it
the times you were left astounded
compounded with disbelief
that you could ever feel this free
your new motif
just being completely
wide-eyed seeing
how each experience brings new meaning
although moments are fleeting
I urge you to keep dreaming
please believe me
this isn't your only chance at happiness

you have no idea how good it can be

to let go of everything that was
required letting go of everything that would be
and letting go of everything that will be
to be able to stand here
free, happily
in the present
of what is
right in front of me

all we have is now

it's written all over my face
I'm illuminated by rays
I embrace this place
happiness
I think I let you go with grace
after grieving the life we built
after letting the pink flowers wilt
I found myself
saying
I don't miss you like I thought I would

MEIGHAN KLIPPENSTEIN

a reminder
some people come into your life
just to rearrange the pieces
if you can believe it
they can inspire a new way of being
you didn't know you needed
I like to think of them as cleaners

remember to say thank you

do you notice it?
when life's magic
subtly yet suddenly
crashes into you
what do you do?

do you feel it?
the difference in the air
the way it fills your lungs
the way it stays in your hair
the way it's laced with enough electricity
to make you believe in synchronicity

do you notice it?

　　　　　　　　　　　　MEIGHAN KLIPPENSTEIN

everything has seasons
everybody has reasons
I know it can be hard to see them
but please believe it
when they say
change is the only way
it might look like it's breaking
but really it's taking new shape
keep looking forward
keep trusting your own word
at the end of the day
everything has reasons
everybody has seasons
they're all just pieces
you can decide
when to leave them behind
when to keep in mind
everything has seasons
and
everybody has reasons

not knowing where we were going
was all we needed to know

letting it unfold

MEIGHAN KLIPPENSTEIN

there are bridges between
what breaks us
what shapes us
what makes us
whole

cross them

some people only show you
who they want to be
finding all the right words
I think they truly do believe
sometimes you find yourself thinking
actions are the missing piece
if life has taught me anything
it's to listen before it turns to grief
remember to breathe
I know it's confusing
but one thing you must believe
is that people will show you who they really are
by the way they leave

MEIGHAN KLIPPENSTEIN

try not to spend much time
wondering why
some people only want to bask
in your light
in your life
for a moment
don't try to hold them
simply let that time together
be golden

let them come
let them go

"*rien est perdu*"
softly spoken words across the table
the gift of insight
I would have missed
had I not been paying attention

nothing is lost

the best part of life

can be opening your hands

to the chance

to risk

to grow

to show yourself you can

stand expanding

in unimagined plans

new favourite moments that came

around corners you never saw coming

I don't wish
for what could be
life has thrown me
too many sharp turns
to ever think such a thing
as wishing
can bring me toward something
I desire

you have to make it happen

MEIGHAN KLIPPENSTEIN

it's so subtle
you barely notice the deep exhale
creating space within
remember this feeling
eyes on the ceiling
these moments
you can't imagine
before they exist
inside of those
seconds, minutes, hours
it's where lifetimes live

a specific space
in no specific place

my definition of home

MEIGHAN KLIPPENSTEIN

there are days I look through my life
revisiting every cord
there are days I find myself at the beginning
searching for an explanation
the pain so blatant
the memories aren't fading
I had no choice in making them
there are days I understand
there are days I don't
and there are days
I am reminded
although I cannot alter the cords
I can sever them
my resilience is my own

have you ever caught yourself
selfishly reaching for something
holding it close
deciding it was yours
without stopping to consider
maybe it belongs exactly where it is

not everything needs to come with you

MEIGHAN KLIPPENSTEIN

life won't let me have it all
in my hands at once
it extorts me
forcing me to put something down
before I can hold something else

from time to time
showing up means
choosing yourself
honouring the boundaries
you created
in the understanding
in the knowing
of what you deserve
it means standing knee deep
in the courage you saved for a rainy day
remembering it's okay
with how long it took
to come this far
and remembering
there will always be farther to go

keep going

MEIGHAN KLIPPENSTEIN

I had never really thought much
about being someone
that I might like to know
getting there
meant accepting everything that was
painful and necessary
making room for everything that is
beautiful and new
a chance to understand
once you finally learn
to love who you are
the company you keep
with yourself
can make you laugh
as much as you cry

a blue door
stands before
black and white tiles
to a house that isn't mine
down a street whose name I can never remember
can you picture it
a home
whose walls are filled with books
a single lamp sits near the window
what kind of life lives there
is it full
of feeling
of love
of loss
of light

imagine

I was always waiting
for someone to bring me flowers
it took me a long time
and a lot of heartache
to understand
I was waiting for myself all along
so now I buy myself pink carnations
just because—they light me up
and once they start to wilt
I hang them in the window to dry
like relics
to remind
me

I was waiting for myself all along

Reprinted with permission: first published in
WordWorks 2023 Volume 1

my solace
when it all gets too much
always she is there
everywhere
with her infinite insistence
to keep moving forward
her sacred spaces
her magnificent outside places
they heal me
they heal me

a letter to mother nature

MEIGHAN KLIPPENSTEIN

an ode to the wind

revisiting the healing places where the trees decipher
her language
coming to understand after the second time
that you can in fact hear what she is saying
if you stand still long enough
she will recalibrate the ever-spinning compass that lives
inside of you
she will teach you that everything is transitory

how healing it has been
to be held
supported
seen
in this grieving season
helping me release
everything
I had been
holding onto
too tightly

it was time

what a privilege it is
how we get to be
so many things
in this life

let yourself

there is a certain wonder
the way the resting trees
collect falling snow
how even their bare branches
offer us something beautiful
it is not just their blooming fullness
that reminds us of life
when we think there is nothing left
to look at
how we can lift our eyes
to find
the tiny home sitting high among the branches
showing us
life has many seasons and
how we can't always see
one when we are in the other

keep your head up

MEIGHAN KLIPPENSTEIN

the space in between
who I have been
and who I am becoming
requires me to linger
longer than I'd like to
mourning the person
I don't want to be any more

growth
rips you apart at the seams
hands you the pieces
of your old self
and asks you to try again

some days all it takes
is covering my eyes
to be able to hide
from the loneliness inside
at times it disguises
itself as something else
it's okay to hate
the uncomfortable stages
required of patience
but please don't cave in
the better days are on their way
just wait
just wait
just wait

you'll see

MEIGHAN KLIPPENSTEIN

it's a strange feeling to comprehend
you will never again
be this person
in this exact place
there is no way to retrace
all the versions you've been
all you have is this you
today

I am amazed
the day's finally come
where I hardly think of you
the thought in my head is about
how not every dream comes true
you don't always get to decide
you will find at times
it doesn't matter how hard you try
you must let go of the picture in your mind
let life erase, retrace, replace
embrace all of it
it's teaching you to *gracefully*
abide by the laws of life
I am amazed

MEIGHAN KLIPPENSTEIN

you come
you go
you never know
what will leave a mark
what will be the start
of the next page
of the next chapter that changes
everything

stay open

inhale
open
expand
allow
experience
release
contract
close
exhale
repeat

a necessary cycle

MEIGHAN KLIPPENSTEIN

is it a place to hide behind
does it send shivers down your spine
to think time is not often on our side
things rarely perfectly align
and when they do we seem to find
all the reasons why
the timing isn't right

I think we choose
I think it comes down to follow-through
how much you want it
and what you're willing to do
for the ability to step into
the mindset of all the reasons why
the timing can always be right

life has a subtle way of reminding you
that what you seek will always find you
but when it only gives you a taste of its existence
please think of it as patience paying dividends

PART III

feel the love

I don't believe in chance encounters
I have spent too many days
watching the ocean
return to the shore
with such certainty
without mercy
I think there must only be eternity
for two things so perfectly entwined
and if we are not tied
how else do we continually find
ourselves pulled together again
time after time
always coming back around
like the rise and fall of the tide

the most romantic moment I've ever known:
amongst the mountains
watching the snow
falling
in my favourite place
your arms around me
it was all enthralling

I still think about it

the most valuable things I hold
are things I could never own
a box of hand-written notes
each one
their own version of prose
gifted over a lifetime
oh how sometimes
they became a lifeline
something tangible to remind
that the great romances in this life
already live
inside of our friendships

while my heart was breaking
she called me every morning
to make sure I was waking
encouraging me to keep taking
up space
to create something
from the sadness
I've never known a greater love than this
in the midst of the madness
she had me

the definition of I've got you

MEIGHAN KLIPPENSTEIN

the story I created
was powerful
the love we fabricated
in another life
I think we could have made it
into something beautiful
and it was timely
that I was staring at the sea
with waves crashing in front me
when I heard the echo
of all that I didn't know
about the story I created
about the love we fabricated
and it was in that moment
when I let you go

I think forever
is just every day
put together

Italian wisdom

there is something special
about the way
the arbutus trees
reach toward the sea
with such eloquent conviction
often standing on the precipice
some might mistake it for recklessness
yet all I ever see
is the delicate reflection
of certainty

I was sure I loved you

counting raindrops
am I making the right decision
never have I had such precision
listening to my intuition
it said don't go
I didn't go
and now I know
it was so we could find each other
again

it *was* a love story for the ages

MEIGHAN KLIPPENSTEIN

I hope you let the special people you meet
weave pieces of themselves
into your being
it's a beautiful way to keep them with you
even if they decide to leave

placing the past on paper
carefully choosing each word
required the kind of honesty
that did not come easily
like how my favourite places
slowly became ours
my memories carved your face
into spaces
where it was once just me
reminiscing, I see
your hands holding, warming mine
on every inch of that island
it was a series of moments intertwining
it was terrifying
creating something so beautiful
that time
those places
those memories
they were always meant
for you and me

MEIGHAN KLIPPENSTEIN

we stood there feeling everything fully
and all at once
it overwhelmed
you and I
when our souls spoke without using words
knowing our hearts had heard
each other before

deep soul knowing

if we had kissed one more time
there'd be no denying
we wouldn't have been able to stop
ourselves from falling
forward toward exploring
a future
you recognized it
as we were driving
your hand in mine
I saw it coming
it was so exciting without trying
the only thing
that didn't align
was timing

MEIGHAN KLIPPENSTEIN

how quickly you switched directions
felt like rejection
it wasn't a reflection
of the collection of moments
we created
but they evaporated
before I could have a say in it
it wasn't exaggerated
the chemistry
the contrast
when we collaborated
a huge value add
it went so fast
in fact
I'd do it all again
even knowing how it ends

you filled my cup and then left it in the kitchen

'if you want to write
I will always read'

the first time anyone gifted me
a string of words written so beautifully
though they were temporary
I see it as a treasure
I wasn't meant to keep forever
a moment that keeps me believing
the kind of love I dream of exists

for everything you lost
for everything that lost you
each a lesson
in how life takes
and then replaces
all of the spaces
with a chance to renew
yourself into something better
a malleable being
who now stands there seeing
how it all belongs
how everything you lost
how everything that lost you
each piece
every part
offers you a fresh start
a chance to undo
a chance to say thank you
to everything you lost
to everything that lost you

are you having trouble finding
the kind of love
that exists in your mind
taking chances inside new romances
learning to let it flow on feeling
allowing it to sweep in gleaming
only to have it redirect itself
somewhere else
oh I know it's disappointing
to let that sink in
but I promise what you find
on the other side
is a pleasure to remember

rejection
is just the next step
in the right direction

MEIGHAN KLIPPENSTEIN

it was big energy
when your eyes
locked on mine
unsure of what we would find
but I had a feeling
you were going to be
a very important piece

I was right

I wonder why
in life we find
people who feel just like home
only to have them go
suddenly
unexpectedly
redirecting everything
when I had thought differently
oh the heart
is such a messy thing
I wonder why

I can't wait to find out

MEIGHAN KLIPPENSTEIN

my hand on your slow-beating heart
could've easily been the best part
but the happiness for me
came from my ability to breathe
fully, freely
into who I have always been
me in my element
a moment so relevant
your words never more eloquent
that morning by the beach
it was so simple
you seeing me
carrying flowers down the street

there are many reasons why
trusting the timing of your life
can be hard sometimes
patience might feel like
nothing is going right
but you never know
it just might be teaching
you exactly how to dig deep
how to keep the peace
inside of your mind
so when nothing is going right
it can still feel like
perpetual motion forward towards
letting it be
a
good
life

MEIGHAN KLIPPENSTEIN

Acknowledgements

This book wouldn't have been created without the people who let me send them endless rough drafts, edits, and final pieces. Your support filled my cup when it I needed it most. You helped me remember why I started and every time I look at these pages, I am reminded of how fortunate I am to be surrounded and loved by such incredible people.

À la vie.
To life.

Thank you for being a part of my story.

About the Author

As a Bodywork Therapist, Meighan Klippenstein
has made a career out of helping people experience a
profound understanding of the body-mind connection.
Connection being at the heart of everything she does,
writing poetry is the thread she weaves through her own
experiences to make sense of the ebbs and flows of life.
"Let It Be A Good Life" is her debut book.
She lives on Vancouver Island.